The Anthony J Zigler Guide to the Galaxies

by Anthony J Zigler (with a little help from Wendy Body)

illustrated by Nick Davies

Welcome, Time Traveller!
My name is Anthony J Zigler
and I invented the amazing
Mark 5 Time Machine.

Your Mark 5 Time Machine can take you anywhere you want to go. It can take you to planets you know about and to planets you don't know about.

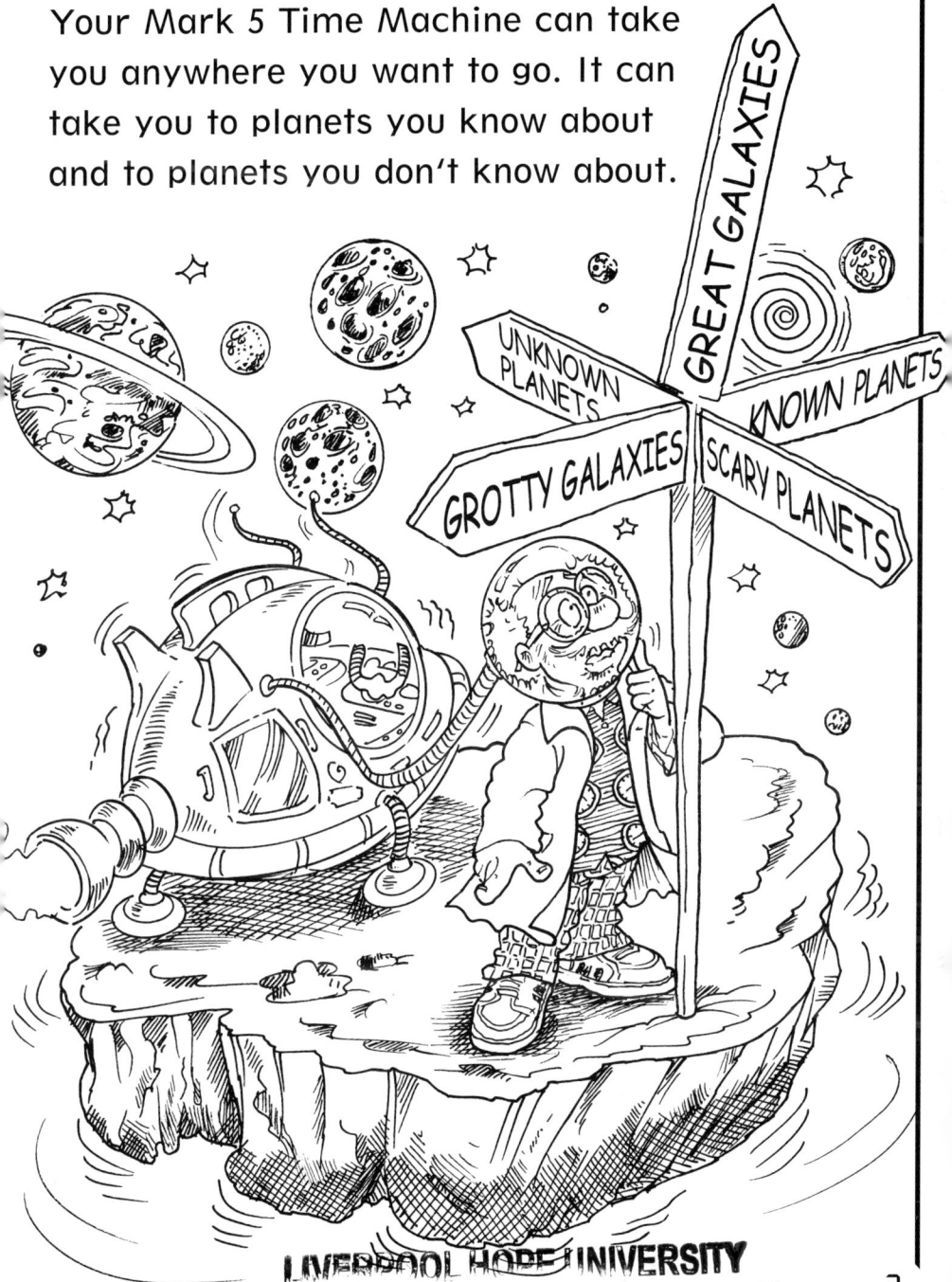

GREAT GALAXIES

UNKNOWN PLANETS

KNOWN PLANETS

GROTTY GALAXIES

SCARY PLANETS

3

But now you can go even faster! All you need is the AJZ Plastic Mega Thrust ... only 99p if you already own a Mark 5 Time Machine.

AJZ PLASTIC
MEGA THRUST
99P
(BATTERIES
NOT INCLUDED)

Fit the AJZ Plastic Mega Thrust to your Mark 5
Time Machine and you can be on the other
side of your Universe in just ten minutes.
But whatever you do, don't go without
'The Anthony J Zigler Guide to the Galaxies' ...

The Anthony J Zigler
Guide to the

Galaxies

5

Asperyn

No, this is not something you take for a bad headache! This is the planet where you will find all the peanut butter mines.

THIS WAY TO THE MINE

I'm sure I'm turning into a peanut!

OFFICIAL TASTER

ZIGLER STAR RATING
★ ★ ★ ★ ★
if you like peanut butter

ZIGLER STAR RATING
○ ○ ○ ○ ○
if you hate peanut butter

Burp

This place is filled with aliens saying, "I beg your pardon!" and "Excuse me!" They are rather boring but at least they have good manners!

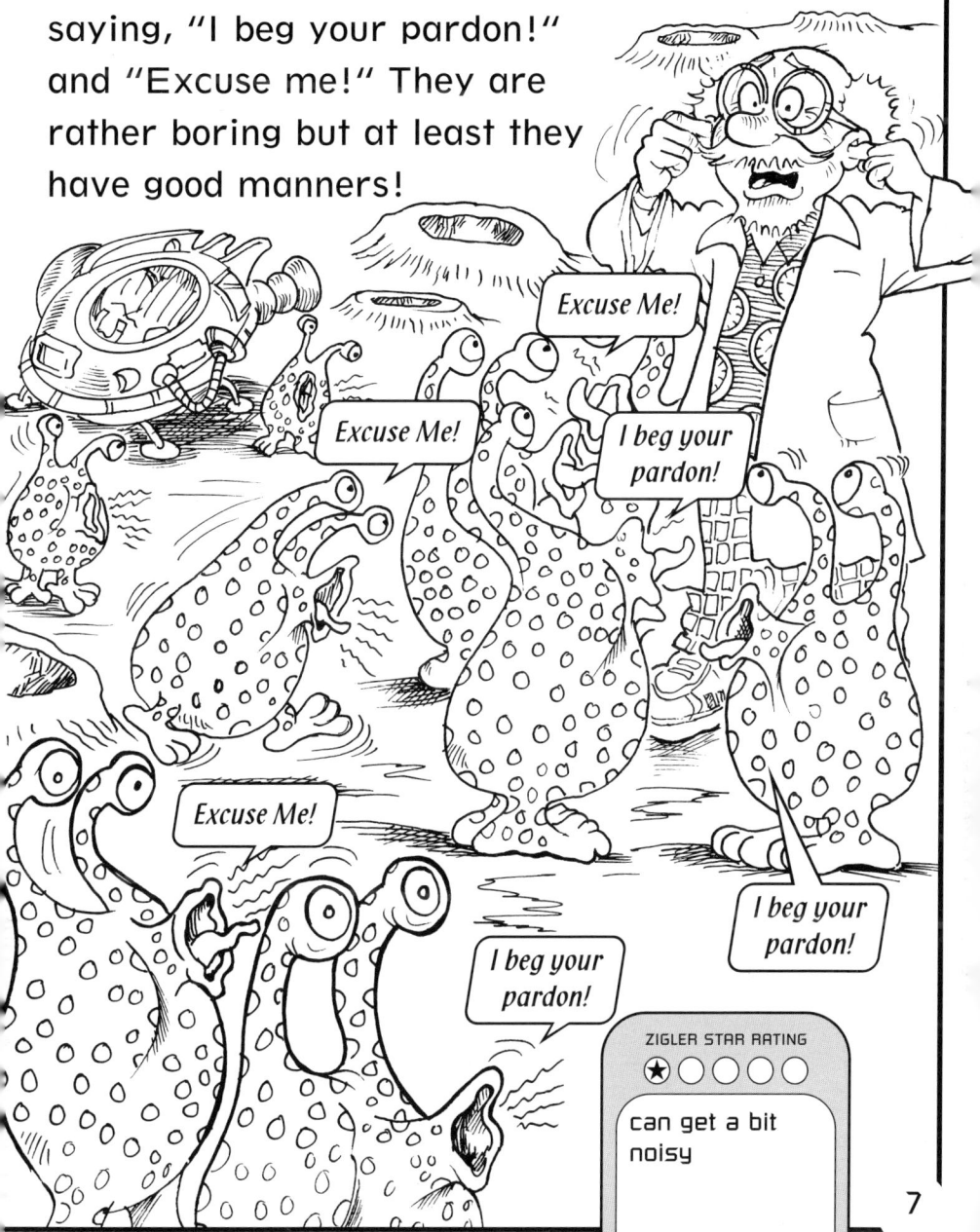

Cavity

The Cavity Galaxy is full of black holes. Fall in a big one and you might never be seen again!

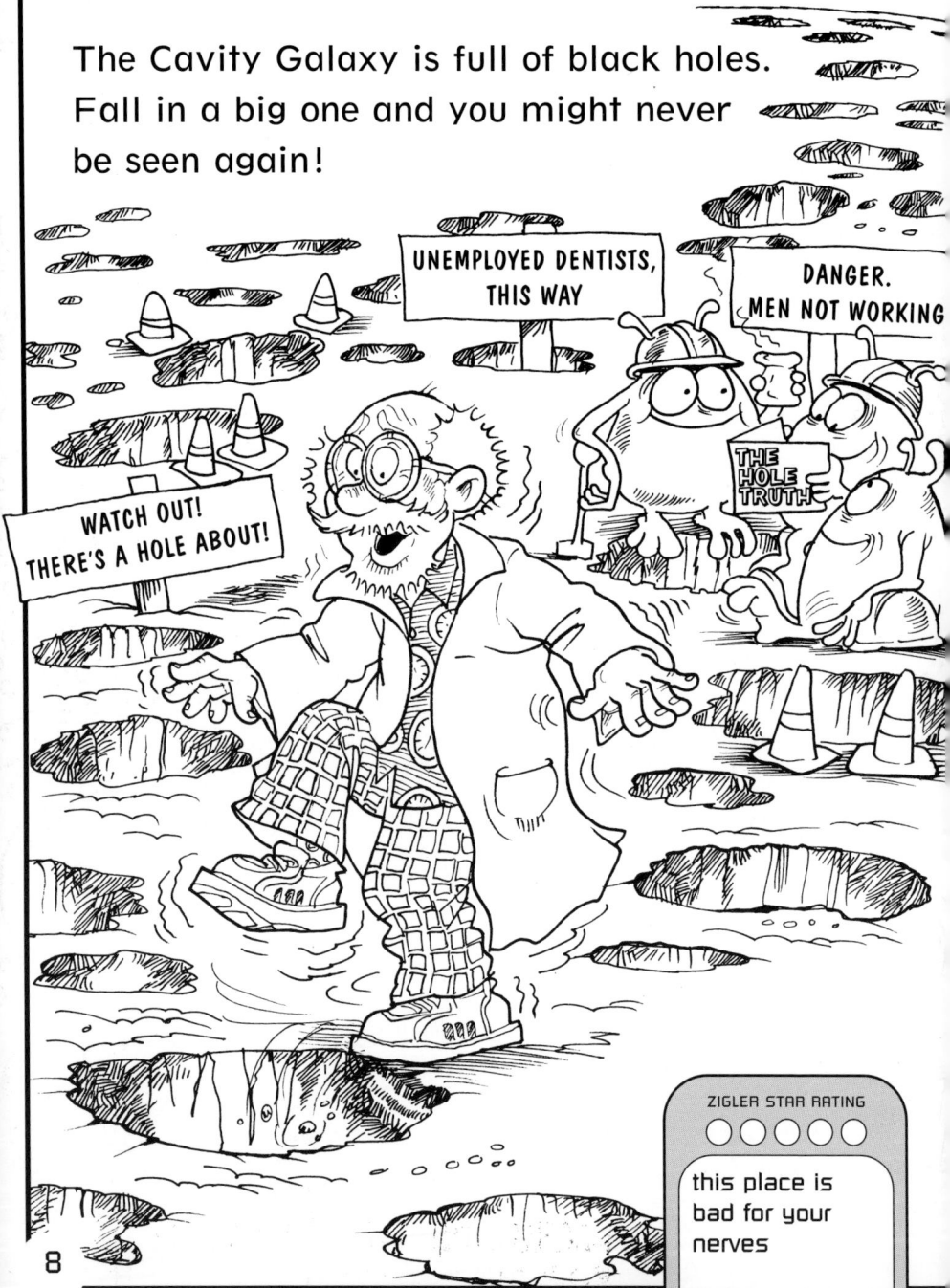

UNEMPLOYED DENTISTS, THIS WAY

DANGER. MEN NOT WORKING

THE HOLE TRUTH

WATCH OUT! THERE'S A HOLE ABOUT!

ZIGLER STAR RATING

this place is bad for your nerves

Decibel

This is THE place to go! It's where they hold the Inter-Galactic Disco Championships. I won it in 2053.

ZIGLER STAR RATING

⭐⭐⭐⭐⭐

wicked!

Eggs-r-us

This planet is famous
for its eggs ...

JELLY EGGS

CHOCOLATE EGGS

BAD EGGS

CHEESE EGGS

EGGSELLENT EGGS

SUGAR EGGS

SPAGHETTI EGGS

ZIGLER STAR RATING

not eggsactly
my favourite
planet – but
almost!

Futuria

Go to this galaxy and you will find out what you will be doing in ten years' time. Don't go if you don't want to know!

You are going to meet a tall dark stranger very soon ...

ZIGLER STAR RATING
★★★★☆

if you have a future!

Gumm

This is the place where aliens go to get their false teeth.

Heeblehare

This is where you will meet the Heebles.
You can't miss them – they've got hairy feet,
blue noses and purple ears.
(They've also got pea-sized brains ...)

Make that pin
not pea ...

PURPLE EARS →

BLUE NOSE →

← HAIRY FEET

ZIGLER STAR RATING
★○○○○

unless you've
got a thing
about purple
ears ...

llastic

This is a very stretchy planet. It stretches from one side of the Nikka galaxy to the other.

ZIGLER STAR RATING
★★○○○

it keeps moving so it's hard to land on it

Joker

Guess who lives here! There are also aliens who tell terrible jokes ...

Where did Batman keep his armies?

Up his sleevies.

ZIGLER STAR RATING

★★★★☆

if you like jokes you'll like this one!

Kilt

This is not the long lost home of the Scots but it is the home of the Tartans.

Me Tartan – you Jane.

ZIGLER STAR RATING
★ ★ ☆ ☆ ☆

you need ear plugs for all that Tartan yelling!

Lockness

The planet Lockness is famous for its monsters.
But you never get to see them.

LOCKNESS
MONSTER
SPOTTING

ZIGLER STAR RATING

⭐◯◯◯◯

a waste of time
as far as
monsters go

Metallic

Don't crash land on this one
– it could be painful!

BOIN-N-N-NG

ZIGLER STAR RATING

★ ○ ○ ○ ○

it gets rusty
when it rains

Nosey

The planets in this galaxy have holes in the middle so that you can see what's happening on the next one.

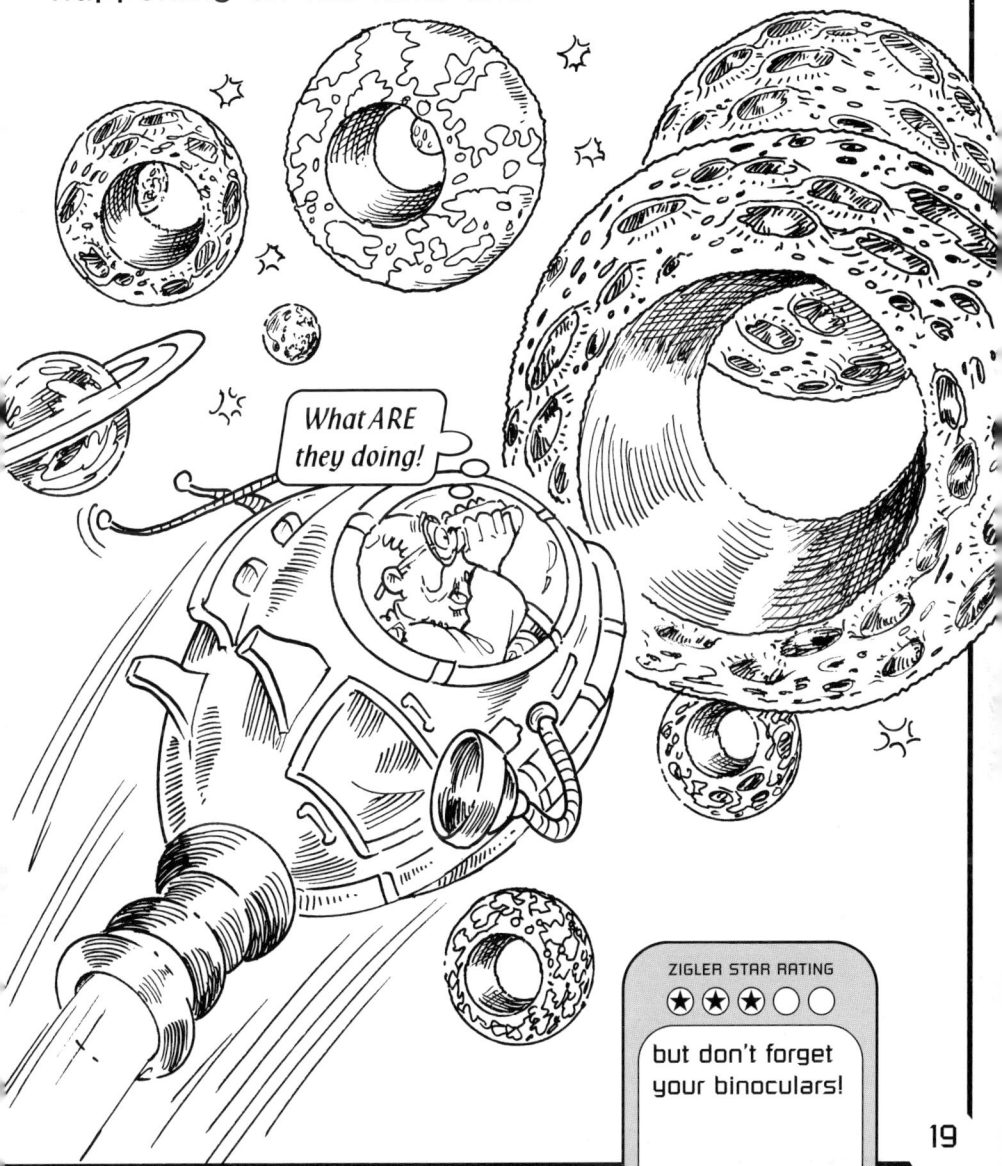

What ARE they doing!

ZIGLER STAR RATING

but don't forget your binoculars!

Octave

This was the home of the famous singer Elvis Parsley.

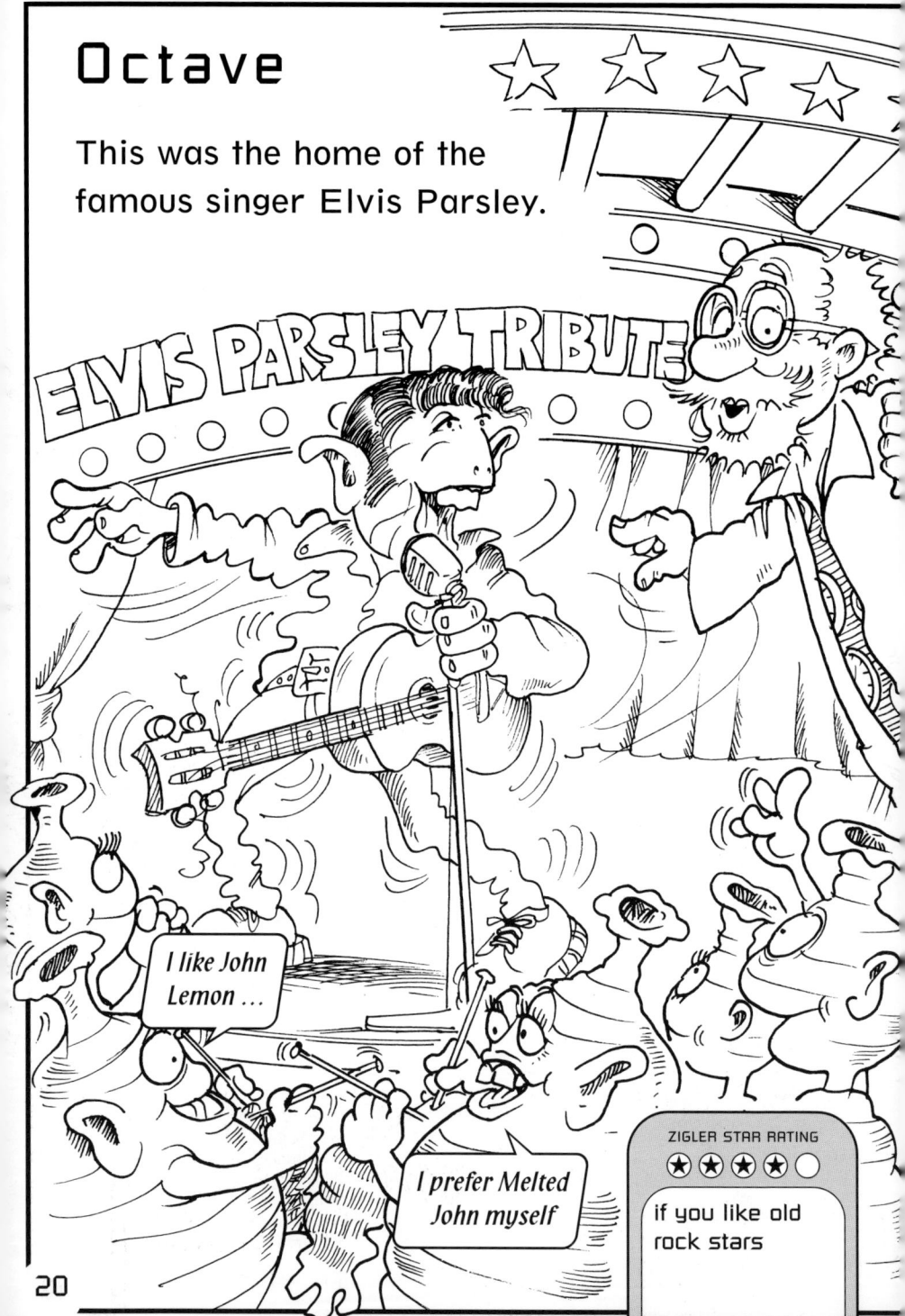

ELVIS PARSLEY TRIBUTE

I like John Lemon …

I prefer Melted John myself

ZIGLER STAR RATING

★★★★☆

if you like old rock stars

Pitts

Turn left just after Octave and you'll find
this planet. My advice is to turn right ...
Pitts really is the pits!

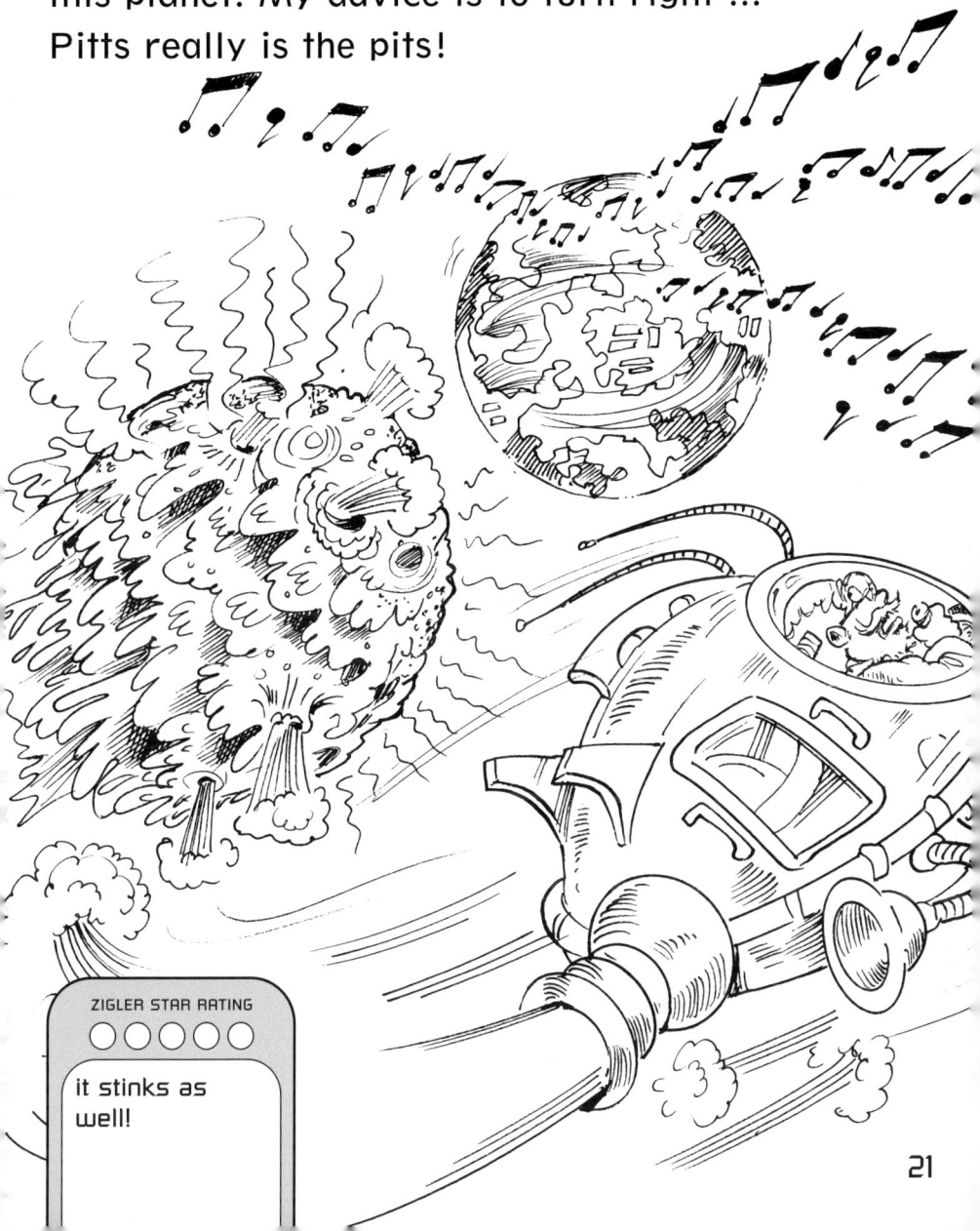

ZIGLER STAR RATING

○○○○○

it stinks as
well!

Quillt

A very soft planet which is a rest home
for the very tired ...

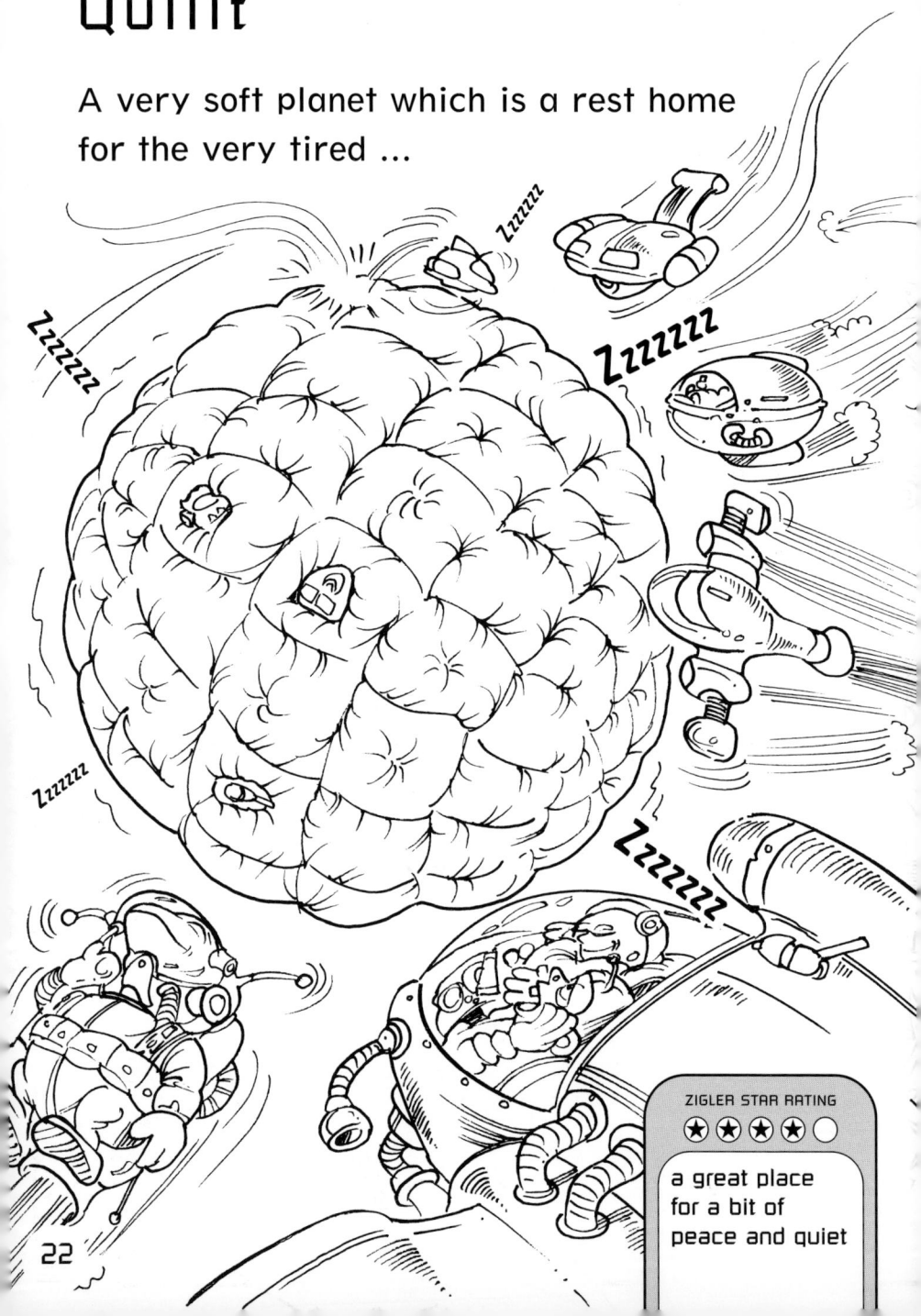

ZIGLER STAR RATING
★★★★☆

a great place
for a bit of
peace and quiet

Roobarb

This planet gets its name from its inhabitants. They go round muttering "Roobar, roobar," all the time. They are not good conversationalists.

ZIGLER STAR RATING

not the place to enlarge your vocabulary

Somewhere

The lost planet of Somewhere
could be anywhere, so if you
find it please let me know!

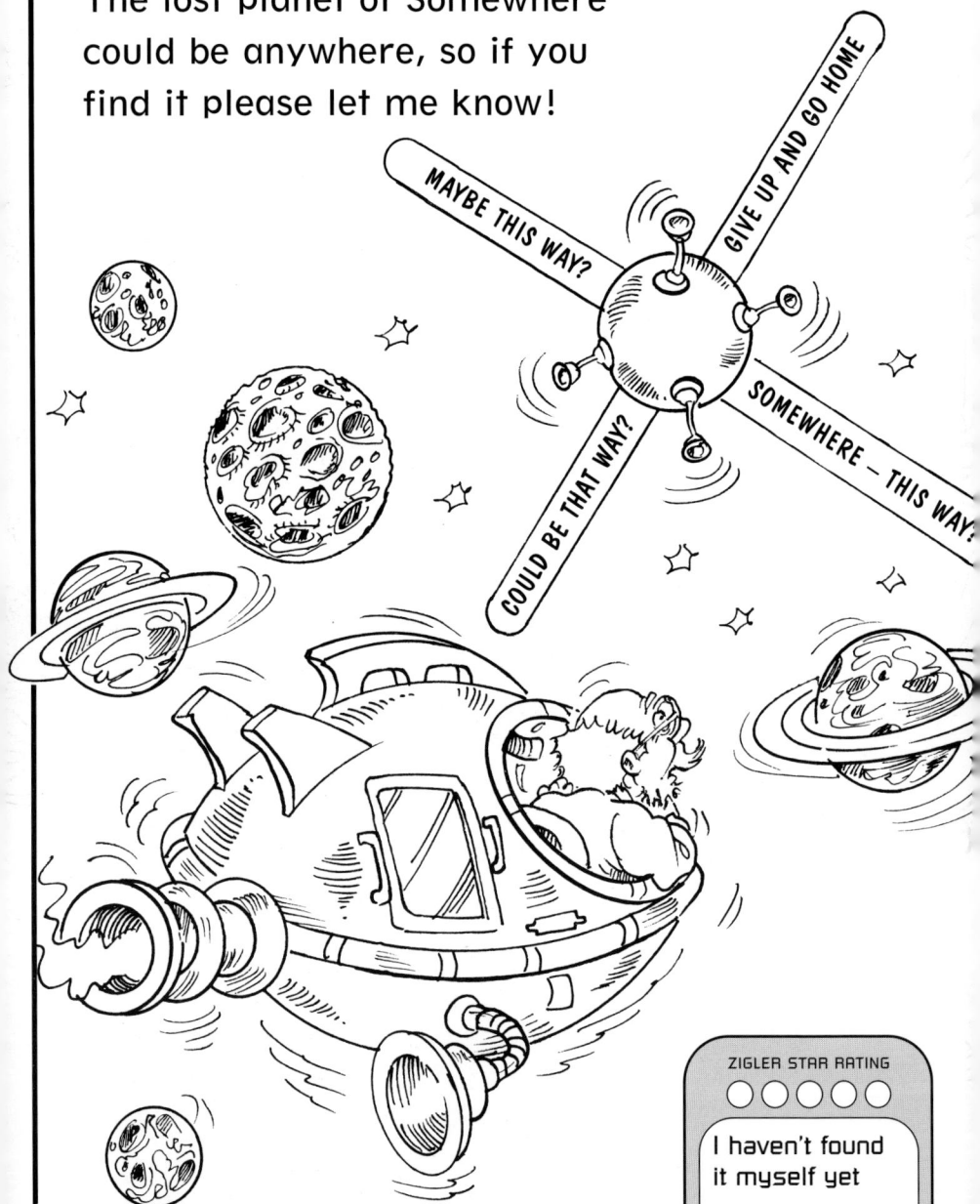

MAYBE THIS WAY?

GIVE UP AND GO HOME

COULD BE THAT WAY?

SOMEWHERE – THIS WAY!

ZIGLER STAR RATING
○○○○○

I haven't found
it myself yet

Teflon

This is a very slippery planet.
Nothing sticks to anything here!

good for
practising
winter sports

25

Unison

Everyone looks exactly the same on Unison. This can make life difficult ...

Aren't you Aunty Nelly?

Are you my dad?

Are you my wife?

Are you my best friend?

ZIGLER STAR RATING

not a good place to have an identity crisis!

Vulcan

This planet does not exist. It was made up
by some chap with pointed ears on the telly.

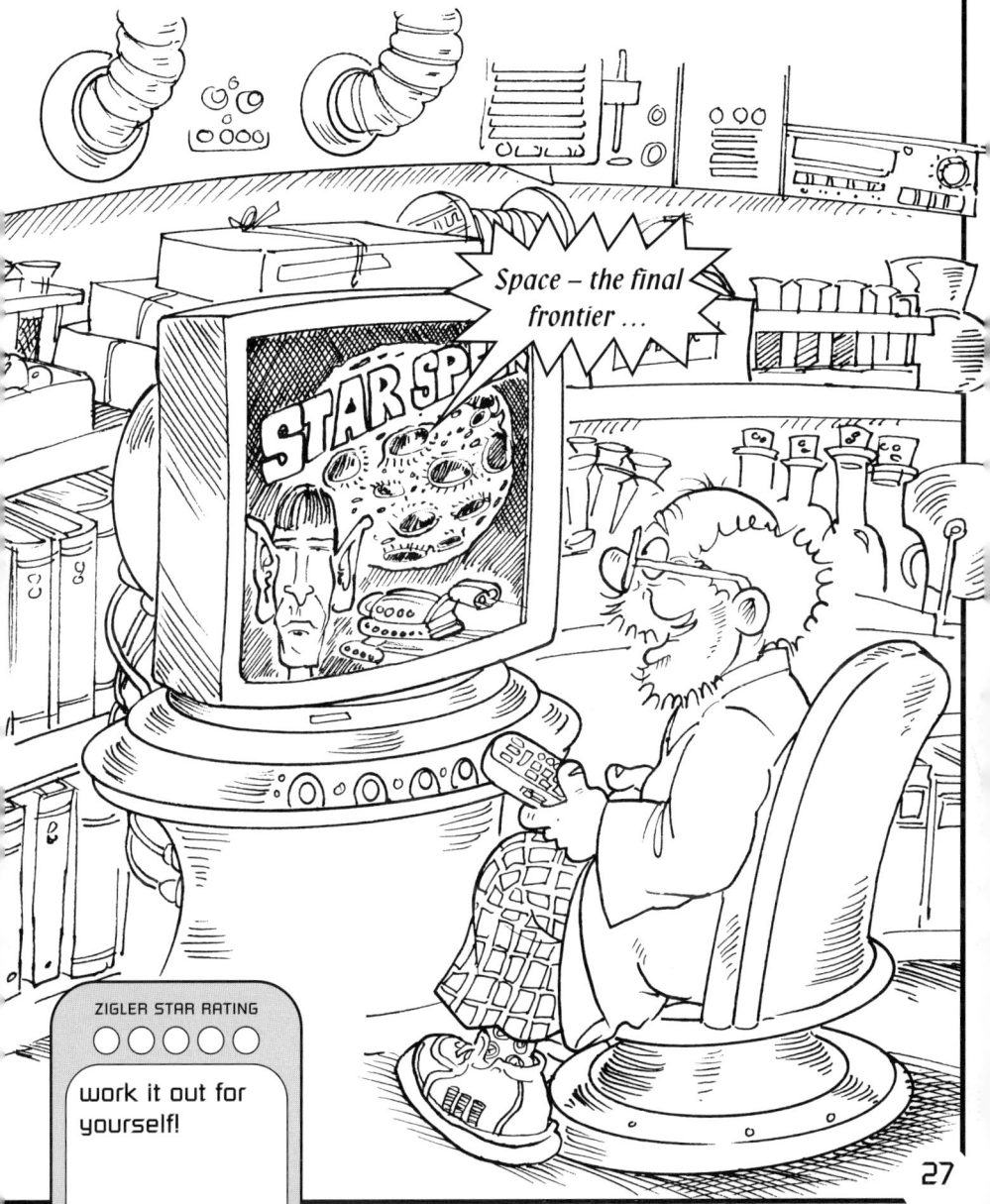

ZIGLER STAR RATING

work it out for
yourself!

Webb

No dotcoms here – just ENORMOUS spiders waiting to eat you!

ZIGLER STAR RATING

Ugh!

X-rai

The inhabitants of this planet can see into your mind so watch what you are thinking!

ZIGLER STAR RATING

Are you sure your teacher doesn't come from this planet?

YAMOP

The YAMOP Galaxy is pretty boring.
This is because YAMOP stands for
Yellow And Made Of Plastic.

yellow plastic

yellow plastic

yellow plastic

yellow plastic

yellow plastic

ZIGLER STAR RATING

but only if you
like yellow!

Ziglerzone

The Duke of Wellington may have given you wellies ... the Earl of Sandwich may have given you two bits of bread and a lump of cheese, but I, Anthony J Zigler have given you the perfect planet!

ZIGLER STAR RATING

★ ★ ★ ★ ★

x 2 Wow!

It can be
whatever you
want it to be!